MW00951828

* WE ARE AMERICA *

Vietnamese Americans

MARGARET C. HALL

Heinemann Library
Chicago, Illinois

Customer Service 888-454-2279

Visit our website at www.heinemannlibrary.com

Created by the publishing team at Heinemann Library
Designed by Roslyn Broder
Photo research by Amor Montes de Oca
Printed and Bound in the United States by Lake Book Manufacturing, Inc.

07 06 05 04 03
10 9 8 7 6 5 4 3 2 1

Library of Congress Cataloging-in-Publication Data
Hall, Margaret, 1947-
    Vietnamese Americans / M.C. Hall.
        p. cm. — (We are America)
    Summary: Discusses conditions in Vietnam, particularly after 1975, that led Vietnamese to leave the country, describes the difficulties these people faced, how they managed to immigrate to the United States and to keep their traditions alive in their new homeland.
    Includes bibliographical references (p.) and index.
    ISBN 1-40340-738-X (lib. bdg.) ISBN 1-40343-139-6 (pbk. bdg.)
    1. Vietnamese Americans—Juvenile literature. 2. Refugees—United States—Juvenile literature. 3. United States—Emigration and immigration—Juvenile literature. 4. Vietnam—Emigration and immigration—Juvenile literature. 5. Vietnamese Americans—Biography—Juvenile literature. 6. Refugees—United States—Biography—Juvenile literature. [1. Vietnamese Americans. 2. Refugees. 3. United States—Emigration and immigration.] I. Title. II. Series.
    E184.V53H35 2003
    973.04'9592—dc21
    2002013102

Acknowledgments
The author and publishers are grateful to the following for permission to reproduce copyright material:
pp. 4, 5, 28, 29 Courtesy of Nan Thi Nguyen; pp. 8, 11, 12, 13 Bettman/Corbis; p. 9 Nik Wheeler; p. 10 Courtesy of The Gerald R. Ford Library; p. 14 U.S. National Archives & Records Administration; p. 15 Earl & Nazima Kowall/Corbis; p. 16 David H. Wells/Corbis; pp. 18, 19 Bob Daemmrich/The Image Works; p. 20 Catherine Karnow/Corbis; pp. 21, 23 Spencer Grant/PhotoEdit, Inc.; p. 22 Tony Freeman/PhotoEdit, Inc.; pp. 24, 25 Robert Lifson/Heinemann Library; p. 26 A. Ramey/PhotoEdit, Inc.; p. 27 Lawrence Migdale

Cover photographs by (foreground) Spencer Grant/Art Directors, (background) Robert Lifson/Heinemann Library

Special thanks to Dr. Joseph Vuong of Tulane University and Christina Tran of Heinemann Library for their comments in preparation of this book and to Tina Nguyen for sharing her story.

Some quotations and material used in this book come from the following sources. In some cases, quotes have been abridged for clarity: pp. 8, 16, 27 *The Vietnamese-Americans* by Tricia Springstubb (Farmington Hills, Mich.: Gale Group, 2001); pp. 12, 15 *The Vietnamese Experience in America* by Paul J. Rutledge (Bloomington, Ind.: Indiana University Press, 1992).

Some words are shown in bold, **like this.** You can find out what they mean by looking in the glossary.

A Vietnamese-American family appears in the foreground on the cover of this book. A photo of Argyle Street in Chicago, Illinois, appears in the background. Argyle Street is home to Chicago's Little Saigon area.

Contents

One Refugee's Story

Nan Thi Nguyen's husband left the country of Vietnam in 1979. He did not agree with Vietnam's government leaders, and he was afraid he would

Nguyen *is a common Vietnamese name. The name is said like the English word* win.

soon be sent to prison. Nan Thi worried until she heard that her husband was safe in Hawaii. She wanted to join her husband, but the Vietnamese government would not let her leave. In 1982, Nan Thi became a **refugee.** She and her son left Vietnam secretly on a small boat with 28 other people.

Nan Thi and her son, Nghia Do, are seen here in front of a refugee camp in 1982.

The refugees headed for the country of Thailand. Twice, they were stopped by fishers, who robbed them. The fishers even took the boat's motor. The refugees made a sail from their clothing. Three weeks later, they were picked up by a ship that belonged to an American oil company. The ship's captain took them to a refugee camp in Thailand.

In 1984, Nan Thi and her husband, On Do, were together again with their son.

We were very lucky. Other people had worse troubles on the way to Thailand.
—Nan Thi Nguyen

Vietnam

France controlled Vietnam for 70 years. In 1945, a war started between France and soldiers in northern Vietnam. It lasted until 1954, when France lost. The Vietnamese people in the north and the south could not agree about who should lead the country. A war started between them. Government leaders in the United States did not like the kind of government that controlled North Vietnam so they sent money and supplies to help the South Vietnamese army. In the 1960s, American soldiers started coming to Vietnam to fight. The war became known as the **Vietnam War.**

This map shows where Vietnam and the United States are located. The countries are shown in orange.

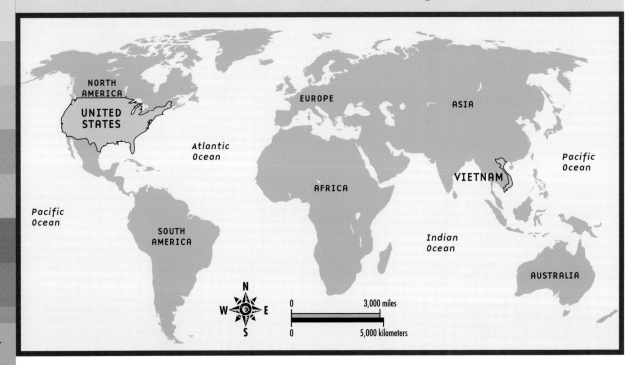

Timeline

1883   Vietnam becomes a French **colony.**

1954   France loses control of Vietnam. Vietnam is divided into North Vietnam and South Vietnam. The Vietnam War starts.

1960   The **Viet Cong** begin to fight against the South Vietnamese government.

         The United States sends soldiers to help the South Vietnamese.

1973   North Vietnam, South Vietnam, and the United States sign an agreement to end the war, but the fighting continues

         United States soldiers begin to leave Vietnam.

1975   North Vietnam takes control of South Vietnam.

The fighting destroyed forests, cities, roads, and crops. Thousands of people were killed. In 1973, North Vietnam, South Vietnam, and the United States signed an agreement saying the Vietnam War was over. American soldiers started to leave Vietnam. However, the Vietnamese armies kept on fighting. By April 1975, the North Vietnamese controlled all of Vietnam.

> Our purpose in Vietnam is . . . just to prevent the forceful conquest of South Vietnam by North Vietnam.
>
> —U.S. President Lyndon B. Johnson, speaking in 1966

The First Refugees

Americans and people who worked in Vietnam for the United States were afraid of the North Vietnamese army. Many people wanted to go to the United States where they would be safe. In April 1975, the South Vietnamese army stopped fighting and headed to the city of Saigon in South Vietnam. Almost one million Vietnamese people traveled with the soldiers. The North Vietnamese army followed them all the way to Saigon.

> We didn't know what to do. We picked up everything in bags and ran . . .
>
> —Ly Thi Tinh, a Vietnamese refugee

Some of these refugees had to leave their homes because their homes had been set on fire.

The Vietnamese people in this photo were trying to climb over the walls of the United States embassy in Saigon, Vietnam.

Refugee or Immigrant?
Both refugees and **immigrants** are people who leave their country to live somewhere else. However, immigrants usually choose to leave. Refugees leave because they face unfair laws, prison, or death if they stay.

By April 25, the Saigon airport was closed because of fighting nearby. American helicopters took some people out of the city. Others lined up outside the United States **embassy,** pleading for help. The United States government helped about 130,000 people leave Vietnam.

These people went to countries that had American **military bases.** At least 50,000 more **refugees** walked or sailed small boats to nearby countries.

Reception Centers

The United States government sent most **refugees** to **immigration** centers at American **military bases** in Asia. From there, the refugees went by airplane to **reception centers** in the United States. There, they had food, places to stay, and doctors to help them. Most refugees stayed in reception centers for about seven months. The centers were crowded. The American food tasted different than Vietnamese food.

On May 5, 1975, Rosalynn Carter, the wife of U.S. President Jimmy Carter, met with Vietnamese children at a reception center in California.

This clown entertained Vietnamese children at a refugee center in the state of Pennsylvania on August 6, 1975.

Refugees with enough money to take care of themselves could leave the reception centers whenever they wanted. Others had to have **sponsors** to help them find jobs and places to live. Churches, **charities,** businesses, and individual persons acted as sponsors.

The people that we are welcoming today . . . are people of talent . . . they are individuals who want freedom, and I believe they will make a contribution now and in the future to a better America.

—U.S. President Gerald Ford, from a May 1975 speech welcoming the first refugees

More Refugees

After 1975, **refugees** continued to leave Vietnam. Some went by land to nearby countries. Others escaped on small, homemade boats. These refugees became known

as "boat people." The boats were poorly made and crowded. Many sank in storms. Robbers attacked and sometimes killed the refugees. Some boats were not allowed to stay once they made it to shore.

The refugees on this boat were from South Vietnam. They were sailing to a refugee center in the country of the Philippines in 1978.

12

These Vietnamese children were among the refugees who had to leave their homes in southern Vietnam.

Refugees who reached a nearby country still had problems. Some governments did not want them to stay. The refugees could not go directly to the United States either. The **reception centers** there were closed. The **United Nations** and the **Red Cross** decided to help. They set up camps in Thailand, Malaysia, Indonesia, Singapore, and Hong Kong. Refugees stayed for weeks, months, or even years before they could go to the United States.

Refugees continued to leave Vietnam even after the war ended. Between 1975 and 1990, about 600,000 Vietnamese refugees came to the United States.

Life in the Camps

Fences made some **refugee** camps seem like prisons. The camps were crowded, too. Many families shared a single, small space. However, there were opportunities in the camps. Refugees could take classes to learn how to speak English. They could learn how to do a new job. In some camps, people had small gardens. There were even camps where refugees ran their own businesses.

In April 1975, an airport in the country of Thailand was crowded with refugees waiting to take flights to the United States.

This photo of Vietnamese refugees shows what it was like for families who lived at the camps.

Most Vietnamese refugees wanted to come to the United States. However, there was a law that said only a small number of **immigrants** could enter the country. In 1980, the U.S. government passed a new law. This law let more refugees come to the United States each year. It also gave money to individual states to help the refugees.

I remember that we had so many people in the camp and no privacy.

—Hue, a refugee in a camp in Malaysia

Facing New Challenges

Government leaders in the United States worried about having too many **refugees** in one place. It would be hard to find houses and jobs for everyone. The government decided to send refugees to cities and towns all over the country. People in these cities or towns offered to be **sponsors.** They helped refugees find homes, schools, doctors, and jobs. Vietnamese people went everywhere from San Francisco to New York to small towns in Iowa.

We are strange to them, but they helped us.
—Vietnamese refugee, speaking about her sponsors

In Virginia, a woman who could speak Vietnamese gave Vietnamese refugees their first look at an American market.

Vietnamese Immigration to the United States

This map shows some of the areas in the United States where Vietnamese people first came to and where many still live today.

The plan to send refugees all over the country caused some problems. Sometimes, only one or two refugees went to the same town. They missed having family members, friends, and other Vietnamese people nearby. There was no one who understood their language or their **culture.** Many refugees were lonely and unhappy in their new homes.

Work and School

The Vietnamese people wanted to find work quickly so they could take care of their families. Some **refugees** had good jobs in Vietnam. But because of differences in language and training, some of them could not work at the same jobs in the United States. Some people who had been teachers delivered newspapers. Doctors drove taxis. Army generals worked in restaurants.

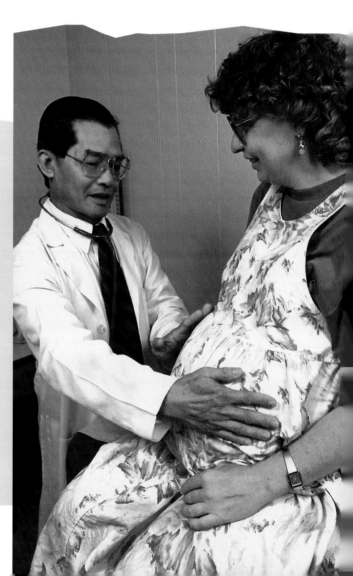

Vietnamese Americans also attended colleges and became scientists and doctors in the United States. This Vietnamese-American doctor was giving a checkup to a woman that is going to have a baby.

This Vietnamese American teaches English to children in Austin, Texas.

The jobs that most Vietnamese **refugees** found in the United States did not pay much. These people needed help from the United States government to pay for food and places to live. Many Vietnamese students had trouble getting used to American schools. The English language was different and new. So was the way students acted. In Vietnamese schools, students were used to listening instead of talking. To them, American schools seemed noisy.

Forming Communities

Many Vietnamese **refugees** moved from small towns to large cities where there were more Vietnamese people. Most went to cities like Los Angeles and San Jose in California. They felt at home there because southern California's land and weather are like Vietnam's. Others went to Washington, D.C., Chicago, and New York. They worked hard to build communities in their cities. They started businesses, opened restaurants, and made homes there.

A neighborhood in Los Angeles, California, is called Little Saigon because of the many Vietnamese shops and restaurants there.

This Vietnamese-American family was shopping in the Little Saigon area of Westminster, California.

Vietnamese-American Populations in the U.S.

Place	Number of Vietnamese Americans
Orange County, California	141,164
San Jose, California	105,259
Los Angeles, California	89,080
Houston, Texas	64,272
Washington, D.C. area	46,791
Oakland, California	32,186
San Diego, California	36,512
Seattle, Washington area	35,742
Chicago, Illinois	17,458
San Francisco, California	17,035
New York, New York	13,874

Source: 2000 United States Census

Vietnamese Americans help others in their communities. They have groups that work with new **immigrants.** Members help newcomers find homes and jobs.

So many Vietnamese Americans live in Garden Grove, California, that it is called Little Saigon. In the 1970s, the area was full of trash and empty buildings. Today, there are homes, temples, and more than 800 restaurants and shops.

Families

To most Vietnamese people, nothing is more important than the family. A family usually includes all relatives. Children, parents, grandparents, great-grandparents, aunts, uncles, and cousins often live together or close to one another. Many Vietnamese-American families work together, too. They run **family businesses** like restaurants, grocery stores, and factories.

This Vietnamese-American woman is playing the guitar for her husband and five children.

This Vietnamese-American grandfather is helping his two grandchildren learn the Vietnamese language.

In **traditional** Vietnamese homes, children are taught that they must work for the good of the family. They also must respect family members who are older than they are. Vietnamese-American parents also teach their children that education is very important. Many adults work during the day and go to school at night. They want their children to study hard, too.

Sean Nguyen was a rice farmer in Vietnam. Today, he helps his family run a computer company in the United States. In 1994, Sean was named Young **Entrepreneur** of the Year by U.S. President Bill Clinton.

Keeping a Culture Alive

In the past, some groups of **immigrants** worked so hard to fit in as Americans that many of their **traditions** were lost. Most Vietnamese immigrants tried to hold on to their language and traditions. This sometimes made it hard for old and young Vietnamese Americans to understand one another. Many older Vietnamese Americans never learned to speak English. Young Vietnamese Americans born in the United States spoke little Vietnamese.

These Vietnamese-American women belong to a club in Chicago that celebrates Vietnamese culture and traditions.

Argyle Street, seen above, is home to a Little Saigon area in Chicago, Illinois. Visitors there can eat Vietnamese food and shop for items from Vietnam.

Today, the Vietnamese **culture** has become a part of American life. Vietnamese-holiday celebrations attract people from other cultures, too. In communities where there are many Vietnamese Americans, there are newspapers printed in Vietnamese. Grocery stores sell vegetables and fruits used in traditional Vietnamese dishes. Vietnamese restaurants are popular with both Vietnamese Americans and other Americans. These restaurants serve traditional foods like bean paste and *pho,* a noodle soup.

Celebrations

Tet, or the **lunar new year,** is the most important Vietnamese holiday. Most Vietnamese people celebrate the holiday for a week. It celebrates the start of a new year and the return of spring. It is also a time to remember the past and think about the future. Tet is celebrated in the United States much like it was in Vietnam. People wear **traditional** clothing and wish each other good luck. Children receive red envelopes filled with money.

These Vietnamese-American girls danced in a festival in Los Angeles, California, that celebrated Tet.

These Vietnamese Americans carried a dragon made out of paper and plastic in a parade for a Tet celebration.

Thousands of people watch fireworks and colorful parades during Tet. It is also a time for games, sports, and dancing. Other traditional holidays celebrated by Vietnamese Americans include Tet Trung Thu, or the Mid-Autumn Festival. Marian Days celebrates the safe arrival of Vietnamese **refugees** in their new land. Celebrating these special days is one way in which Vietnamese Americans bring together their old lives in Vietnam and their new lives in the United States.

> Just because we have a comfortable life in America, we'll not forget our country.
> —Vietnamese-American man

Nan Thi's Story Continues

The Nguyen family is seen here in 2002.

After Nan Thi Nguyen and her son reached a camp in Thailand, they wanted to leave for the United States. But the government of Thailand did not make it easy for **refugees** to leave. There were many rules to follow and papers to fill out. However, Nan Thi was hopeful. She got letters from her husband in Hawaii. He sent money to help Nan Thi and their son in the camp. He worked to find a way to bring his family to the United States.

> I am happy in the United States. My son went to college. He has a good job. My daughter is in college, too.
>
> —Nan Thi Nguyen

In 1984, after two years in Thailand, Nan Thi and her son were finally able to leave. They took an airplane to Honolulu, Hawaii. Nan Thi's husband was waiting for them at the airport.

Today, Nan Thi uses an American name—Tina. She lives in Lake Mary, Florida, with her husband and children. Tina is happy that her children have been able to go to school. Like many Vietnamese Americans, she misses Vietnam but appreciates the freedom she has in her new home.

The son who came with Nan Thi from Vietnam is on the far right in this photo. The photo shows the family outside of their home in Florida.

Vietnamese Immigration Chart

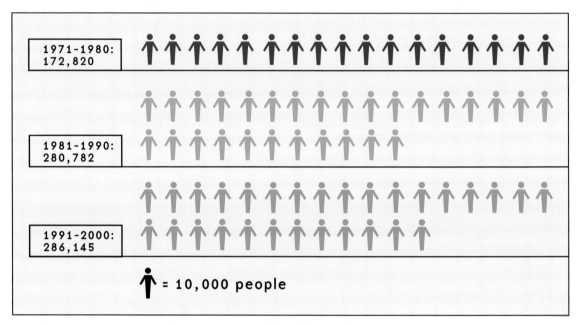

1971–1980: 172,820	
1981–1990: 280,782	
1991–2000: 286,145	

♀ = 10,000 people

*Vietnamese people continued to **immigrate** to the United States in the 1990s.*

Source: U.S. Immigration and Naturalization Service

More Books to Read

Benoit, Susannah. *I Am Vietnamese American.* New York: Rosen Publishing, 1998.

Roop, Peter, and Connie Roop. *Vietnam.* Chicago: Heinemann Library, 1998.

Springstubb, Tricia. *The Vietnamese-Americans.* Farmington Hills, Mich.: Gale Group, 2001.

Willoughby, Douglas. *The Vietnam War.* Chicago: Heinemann Library, 2001.

Glossary

charity organization that works to help people rather than to make money

colony country or territory that is owned or ruled by another country

culture ideas, skills, arts, and way of life for a certain group of people

embassy building where officials of one country live and work in a different country

entrepreneur person who starts his or her own business

family business business owned and run by members of a family

immigrate to come to a country to live there for a long time. A person who immigrates is an immigrant.

lunar new year year that starts sometime between January 20 and February 20 when the second new moon appears. A new moon is when the dark side of the moon is facing the earth.

military base place where a country keeps people and supplies used for defending itself

reception center place set up for Vietnamese refugees just arriving in the United States

Red Cross international organization formed to ease and prevent human suffering worldwide

refugee person who leaves his or her native country to escape war or danger

sponsor person who promises to support others with money, time, and advice

tradition belief or practice handed down through the years from one generation to the next

United Nations international organization formed in 1945 to keep peace and security in the world

Viet Cong group in South Vietnam that fought against its own government with the support of North Vietnam's army

Vietnam War war from 1955 to 1975 between North and South Vietnam for control of the country. The United States fought for South Vietnam, but North Vietnam won control.

Index